# ADHD at Work

## How to Survive in a Neurodiverse Workplace

by

Samuel J. Martinez

# Table of Content

Success Stories: Inspirational Journeys of ADHD Professionals

# Chapter 1

## Understanding ADHD in the Workplace

**Introduction**

Attention Deficit Hyperactivity Disorder (ADHD) is a neurodevelopmental disorder that affects individuals across the lifespan. While it is often associated with difficulties in academic settings, its impact extends into the professional realm as well. This chapter delves into the intricacies of ADHD in the workplace, shedding light on the unique challenges faced by individuals with ADHD and highlighting the strengths that often accompany this condition.

**Understanding ADHD**

ADHD is characterized by persistent patterns of inattention, hyperactivity, and impulsivity. There are three subtypes of ADHD: predominantly inattentive presentation, predominantly hyperactive-impulsive presentation, and combined presentation. Each subtype presents its own set of challenges and strengths in a professional environment.

## Prevalence in the Workplace

ADHD is more common in the workplace than many might realize. According to the Centers for Disease Control and Prevention (CDC), approximately 8.4% of adults have ADHD. This prevalence underscores the importance of understanding how ADHD can manifest in professional settings and how employers can create an inclusive environment.

## Challenges in the Workplace

### Executive Functioning

Individuals with ADHD often struggle with executive functions, which include skills such as organization, time management, and task initiation. These challenges can lead to difficulties in meeting deadlines, staying on task, and managing multiple responsibilities simultaneously.

### Distraction and Impulsivity

The workplace is often a bustling environment, and individuals with ADHD may find it challenging to filter out distractions. Moreover, impulsivity can lead to hasty decision-making, potentially affecting the quality of work and relationships with colleagues.

## Time Management

Time management is a critical skill in any professional setting, and it is an area where individuals with ADHD may face significant hurdles. Procrastination and difficulty estimating the time required for tasks can lead to a cycle of stress and last-minute efforts.

## Social Interactions

Building and maintaining professional relationships require effective communication and social skills. Individuals with ADHD may struggle with these aspects, leading to misunderstandings, conflict, and potential isolation within the workplace.

## Stigma and Misunderstanding

Despite increased awareness, there is still a degree of stigma surrounding ADHD. Misunderstandings about the disorder can result in negative perceptions of affected individuals, impacting their self-esteem and professional growth.

Leveraging Strengths

While ADHD poses its set of challenges, it is crucial to recognize and harness the strengths that often accompany this condition. Individuals with ADHD can bring unique perspectives and qualities to the workplace.

Creativity and Innovation

The hyperactive thought patterns of individuals with ADHD can contribute to creativity and innovation. Their ability to think outside the box and make connections that others might overlook can be valuable in problem-solving and brainstorming sessions.

Hyperfocus

Contrary to the common perception of distractibility, individuals with ADHD can experience hyperfocus, a state where they become intensely absorbed in a task. When channeled effectively, this hyperfocus can result in heightened productivity and the ability to produce high-quality work.

Adaptability

The dynamic nature of ADHD can foster adaptability. Individuals with ADHD often excel in situations that require quick thinking and the ability to pivot in response to changing circumstances, making them valuable assets in fast-paced work environments.

High Energy Levels

Hyperactivity, a hallmark of ADHD, can translate into high energy levels. While it may pose challenges in some contexts, this energy can be channeled into enthusiasm and a proactive approach to tasks, driving team momentum.

Strategies for Workplace Success

Accommodations and Flexibility

Creating an inclusive workplace involves recognizing and accommodating the unique needs of individuals with ADHD. Flexible work schedules, remote work options, and clear communication channels can help individuals navigate their work responsibilities more effectively.

Time Management Tools

Introducing time management tools and techniques can assist individuals with ADHD in organizing their tasks and meeting deadlines. Calendar apps, reminders, and project management software can be instrumental in promoting a structured work routine.

Clear Communication

Promoting open and clear communication is essential for fostering positive workplace relationships. Providing feedback in a constructive manner and ensuring that expectations are communicated explicitly can help individuals with ADHD thrive in their roles.

## Skill Development

Offering training and support in areas such as organization, time management, and social skills can empower individuals with ADHD to overcome challenges and enhance their professional growth. Workshops and coaching programs tailored to their needs can make a significant impact.

## Mental Health Support

Recognizing the potential impact of ADHD on mental health, employers should prioritize creating an environment that supports overall well-being. Access to mental health resources, counseling services, and a culture that destigmatizes seeking help can contribute to a healthier and more productive workforce.

Ultimately, understanding ADHD in the workplace is a multifaceted endeavor that involves acknowledging both the challenges and strengths associated with the condition. When we implement supportive strategies and recognize the unique contributions of individuals with ADHD, workplaces can harness the diverse talents of their employees, ultimately leading to a more vibrant and successful professional community.

# Chapter 2

## Navigating Office Dynamics: A Neurodiverse Perspective

Introduction

As workplaces continue to recognize the importance of diversity and inclusion, the concept of neurodiversity has gained prominence. Neurodiversity acknowledges and values the diversity of neurological experiences, including conditions such as ADHD. Therefore, this chapter will explore the nuances of navigating office dynamics from a neurodiverse perspective, providing tips and strategies for individuals with ADHD to not only cope with challenges but also thrive in an environment that embraces neurodiversity.

## Accepting Neurodiversity

### Shifting Perspectives

To create an inclusive workplace, it is paramount for both employers and colleagues to shift their perspectives and embrace neurodiversity. Rather than viewing ADHD as a hindrance, recognizing it as a unique way of thinking can lead to a more supportive and collaborative work environment.

### Fostering Understanding

Educating colleagues about ADHD and neurodiversity is key to fostering understanding. Workshops, training sessions, and open discussions can help dispel myths and misconceptions, creating a workplace culture that appreciates and values differences.

Tailoring Workspaces for Neurodiversity

## Flexible Work Arrangements

Flexible work arrangements, such as remote work options or adjustable schedules, can provide individuals with ADHD the autonomy to structure their work environment in a way that enhances their productivity. This flexibility allows for better management of attention and energy levels.

## Sensory Considerations

Sensory sensitivities are common in individuals with ADHD. Employers can create a neurodiverse-friendly workspace by considering factors such as lighting, noise levels, and seating arrangements. Providing options for noise-cancelling headphones or quiet spaces can be particularly beneficial.

## Personalized Workstations

Allowing individuals to personalize their workstations can create a sense of comfort and familiarity. This may include incorporating fidget tools, specific desk setups, or other elements that help individuals with ADHD feel more at ease and focused in their work environment.

## Effective Time Management

## Utilizing Time Blocking

Time blocking involves allocating specific blocks of time to different tasks. This technique can help individuals with ADHD manage their time more effectively by creating a structured schedule and reducing the likelihood of procrastination.

## Prioritizing Tasks

Breaking down tasks into smaller, manageable steps and prioritizing them can prevent individuals with ADHD from feeling overwhelmed. Setting realistic goals and deadlines can contribute to a sense of accomplishment and sustained motivation.

## Implementing Routines

Establishing consistent routines can be a powerful tool for individuals with ADHD. Routines create a sense of predictability and stability, making it easier to transition between tasks and maintain focus throughout the workday.

Enhancing Communication Skills

Clear and Direct Communication

Encouraging clear and direct communication is essential for neurodiverse individuals. Colleagues and supervisors can provide instructions and feedback in a straightforward manner, avoiding ambiguity and reducing the risk of misunderstandings.

Utilizing Written Communication

In addition to verbal communication, written communication can serve as a valuable tool for individuals with ADHD. Email, instant messaging, and project management tools allow for information to be conveyed in a format that can be revisited and referenced as needed.

Seeking Feedback

Regular feedback sessions can help individuals with ADHD understand their strengths and areas for improvement. Constructive feedback, provided in a supportive manner, facilitates professional growth and enhances workplace relationships.

Building Strong Professional Relationships

Networking Strategies

Building professional relationships is a crucial aspect of career development. Individuals with ADHD can benefit from networking strategies that play to their strengths, such as attending smaller, more focused events, and using online platforms to connect with colleagues and peers.

## Social Skills Training

For those who find social interactions challenging, participating in social skills training can be beneficial. These programs can provide practical strategies for navigating social situations and building meaningful connections with colleagues.

## Advocating for Support

In a neurodiverse workplace, advocating for the support needed is essential. Individuals with ADHD should feel empowered to communicate their needs to supervisors and colleagues, whether it's related to work accommodations, communication preferences, or additional resources.

## Coping with Stress and Overstimulation

Stress Management Techniques

Stress is a universal aspect of the workplace, and individuals with ADHD may be particularly susceptible to its effects. Employing stress management techniques such as mindfulness, deep breathing exercises, or brief breaks can help maintain mental well-being.

Recognizing Overstimulation Triggers

Understanding personal triggers for overstimulation is crucial. This awareness allows individuals with ADHD to proactively manage their environment and implement strategies to mitigate the impact of overstimulation, such as taking short breaks or finding a quiet space.

Building a Support System

Creating a support system within the workplace can provide individuals with ADHD a sense of community. This may involve connecting with colleagues who understand their neurodiversity, participating in employee resource groups, or seeking mentorship from experienced professionals.

## Professional Development and Growth

### Continuing Education

Continuous learning and professional development are essential components of career growth. Individuals with ADHD can leverage their natural curiosity and enthusiasm by exploring opportunities for training, workshops, and skill-building programs within their field.

Setting Career Goals

Establishing clear career goals and objectives provides a roadmap for professional development. Breaking down long-term goals into manageable steps and celebrating achievements along the way can contribute to a sense of purpose and fulfillment.

Accepting Neurodiversity Initiatives

Getting involved in neurodiversity initiatives within the workplace can be both personally and professionally rewarding. Individuals with ADHD can contribute their unique perspectives to these efforts, advocating for inclusivity and promoting awareness.

# Chapter 3

## Building a Supportive Work Environment

## Introduction

Creating a supportive work environment is essential for bringing about the success and well-being of all employees, including those with ADHD. Employers and colleagues play a pivotal role in shaping the workplace culture and ensuring that it accommodates the diverse needs of neurodiverse individuals. This chapter explores practical advice for building a supportive work environment that empowers individuals with ADHD to thrive.

## Cultivating an Inclusive Culture

### Embracing Diversity and Neurodiversity

An inclusive workplace begins with a culture that embraces diversity in all its forms. Employers should actively promote an environment where neurodiversity is not only accepted but celebrated. By fostering a culture of inclusivity, organizations set the foundation for employees with ADHD to feel valued and understood.

Educating the Workforce

Education is a powerful tool in creating an inclusive workplace. Employers can provide training sessions and resources to help employees understand ADHD and neurodiversity. These initiatives dispel myths, reduce stigma, and promote empathy, fostering a greater understanding of the unique strengths and challenges that individuals with ADHD bring to the workplace.

Implementing Workplace Accommodations

Flexible Work Arrangements

Recognizing the diverse needs of employees with ADHD, employers should consider implementing flexible work arrangements. This may include options such as remote work, flexible hours, or compressed workweeks. Providing flexibility allows individuals with ADHD to manage their workload in a way that aligns with their unique attention and energy patterns.

Workspace Adjustments

Making simple adjustments to the physical workspace can have a significant impact on the comfort and productivity of individuals with ADHD. Employers should consider factors such as lighting, noise levels, and seating arrangements. Providing options for adjustable desks or quiet workspaces can accommodate the sensory needs of neurodiverse employees.

## Assistive Technologies

The integration of assistive technologies can enhance the work experience for individuals with ADHD. Employers should explore and invest in tools such as task management apps, noise-cancelling headphones, and organizational software to support employees in managing their tasks and maintaining focus.

## Clear Communication Strategies

### Establishing Open Lines of Communication

Creating an open and communicative workplace is crucial. Employers should encourage employees to express their needs and preferences, including those related to ADHD. Establishing open lines of communication ensures that potential challenges are addressed proactively, fostering a collaborative and supportive environment.

## Providing Clear Instructions

When giving instructions or conveying information, clarity is key. Employers and colleagues should aim to provide clear and concise instructions, avoiding ambiguity. This practice benefits all employees and is particularly helpful for individuals with ADHD who may thrive on straightforward communication.

## Encouraging Written Communication

In addition to verbal communication, written communication can be valuable. Important information, instructions, and updates can be shared through email, messaging platforms, or project management tools. This allows individuals with ADHD to revisit and reference information as needed, reducing the risk of miscommunication.

## Establishing Supportive Policies

### Accommodation Policies

Explicit policies regarding accommodations for neurodiverse individuals, including those with ADHD, should be established. Employers should communicate these policies clearly, ensuring that employees are aware of the available support mechanisms and feel comfortable requesting accommodations when needed.

### Mental Health Initiatives

Recognizing the intersection of ADHD and mental health, employers should implement mental health initiatives. These can include employee assistance programs, counseling services, and awareness campaigns. Fostering a workplace culture that prioritizes mental well-being benefits all employees and contributes to a supportive atmosphere.

## Neurodiversity Hiring Programs

Implementing neurodiversity hiring programs is a proactive step toward creating an inclusive workplace. By actively recruiting and supporting neurodiverse individuals, employers not only enrich their talent pool but also send a clear message that diversity and inclusion are core values of the organization.

## Training and Sensitization Programs

## Sensitization Training for Colleagues

Organizing sensitization training for colleagues is an effective way to promote understanding and empathy. These sessions can cover topics such as ADHD, its manifestations, and strategies for effective collaboration. Increased awareness helps create a more supportive and harmonious work environment.

## Managerial Training

Managers play a pivotal role in creating a supportive work environment. Providing managerial training on neurodiversity and ADHD equips leaders with the knowledge and skills to effectively manage and support neurodiverse team members. This includes understanding individual needs, offering constructive feedback, and implementing accommodations.

## Peer Mentorship Programs

Establishing peer mentorship programs connects neurodiverse individuals with colleagues who can provide support and guidance. Peer mentors can share experiences, offer coping strategies, and help neurodiverse employees navigate workplace challenges. This initiative fosters a sense of community and solidarity within the organization.

## Promoting Work-Life Balance

### Encouraging Breaks

Regular breaks throughout the workday can be particularly beneficial for individuals with ADHD. Encouraging employees to take short breaks to recharge and refocus can enhance overall productivity and well-being. Employers should communicate a culture that values the importance of breaks for everyone.

## Flexible Leave Policies

Flexible leave policies allow employees to manage their work and personal responsibilities more effectively. Understanding that individuals with ADHD may encounter periods of heightened stress, providing the option for flexible leave arrangements can contribute to a healthier work-life balance.

## Time-Off for Mental Health

Recognizing the impact of ADHD on mental health, employers should destigmatize taking time off for mental health reasons. Acknowledging the importance of mental well-being and allowing employees to prioritize self-care contributes to a positive workplace culture.

Celebrating Achievements and Contributions

Recognition Programs

Implementing employee recognition programs is a powerful way to celebrate the achievements and contributions of all employees. Acknowledging the unique strengths and successes of neurodiverse individuals reinforces their value within the organization and promotes a positive and inclusive atmosphere.

Inclusive Team Building Activities

Organizing team-building activities that are inclusive and considerate of diverse needs promotes camaraderie among colleagues. Employers should ensure that team-building events are designed to accommodate individuals with ADHD, fostering a sense of belonging and teamwork.

Employee Resource Groups

Establishing Employee Resource Groups (ERGs) focused on neurodiversity can provide a platform for individuals with ADHD to connect, share experiences, and advocate for supportive policies. ERGs contribute to a sense of community and provide valuable insights to employers seeking to create an inclusive workplace.

Therefore, recognizing and valuing the unique perspectives and contributions of individuals with ADHD enhances overall team dynamics, fosters innovation, and contributes to the success of the organization as a whole. As workplaces continue to evolve, accepting neurodiversity is not just a moral imperative—it is a strategic decision that positions organizations at the forefront of diversity and inclusion, leading to a more resilient, empathetic, and successful workplace.

# Chapter 4

## Time Management Strategies for ADHD Professionals

**Effective Techniques for Managing Time, Staying Organized, and Meeting Deadlines Despite the Challenges of ADHD**

Time management is an important skill in any professional setting, and individuals with ADHD often face unique challenges in this area. Distractions, impulsivity, and difficulty with organization can make it particularly challenging for ADHD professionals to meet deadlines and maintain productivity. This chapter will therefore examine effective time management strategies tailored to the specific needs of individuals with ADHD, providing practical techniques to enhance organizational skills and optimize productivity in the workplace.

Understanding ADHD and Time Management Challenges

Executive Functioning Impacts

ADHD is closely associated with executive functioning deficits, which include difficulties in areas such as planning, organization, and time management. Professionals with ADHD may find it challenging to initiate tasks, prioritize responsibilities, and estimate the time required for various activities.

Distraction and Hyperfocus

The distractibility associated with ADHD can lead to difficulties in staying on task. On the flip side, individuals with ADHD may also experience hyperfocus—an intense concentration on a specific task to the exclusion of everything else—which can lead to challenges in shifting attention when needed.

## Procrastination

Procrastination is a common challenge for individuals with ADHD. Difficulty starting tasks, coupled with a tendency to underestimate the time needed to complete them, can result in last-minute rushes and increased stress.

## Effective Time Management Strategies

## Utilizing Time Blocking

Time blocking involves allocating specific blocks of time to different tasks or categories of tasks. This technique can help individuals with ADHD create a structured schedule and allocate sufficient time to various responsibilities. It enhances focus by dedicating specific periods to specific activities, reducing the likelihood of distractions.

1. Prioritize Tasks: Start by listing tasks in order of importance. Break down larger tasks into smaller, more manageable steps. This allows for a clearer understanding of priorities and helps prevent feeling overwhelmed.

2. Allocate Time: Assign specific time blocks to different tasks based on their priority. Be realistic about the time needed for each activity. Overestimating time can help account for unforeseen interruptions or delays.

3. Use Visual Aids: Create a visual representation of your schedule using tools like calendars or planners. Color-coding tasks or using visual cues can make the schedule more engaging and easier to follow.

4. Include Breaks: Recognize the importance of breaks in maintaining focus. Schedule short breaks between tasks to recharge and prevent burnout. These breaks can serve as an opportunity to transition between activities.

**Setting Realistic Goals**

1. SMART Goals:

Employ the SMART criteria—Specific, Measurable, Achievable, Relevant, and Time-bound—when setting goals. This approach helps in creating clear and attainable objectives, providing a roadmap for task completion.

2. Break Tasks Into Steps: Divide larger tasks into smaller, more manageable steps. This not only makes the overall task seem less daunting but also allows for a sense of accomplishment at each completed step.

3. Focus on Progress, Not Perfection: Shift the focus from achieving perfection to making progress. Recognize that tasks don't always have to be flawless, and completing them within a reasonable timeframe is a significant achievement.

Implementing Routines

1. Morning and Evening Routines: Establishing consistent morning and evening routines can provide a structured start and end to the day. Routines help create a sense of predictability, making it easier to transition between work and personal life.

2. Task-specific Routines: Develop routines for specific tasks or types of work. For instance, create a routine for responding to emails, preparing for meetings, or starting a new project. This helps in streamlining processes and reducing decision fatigue.

Utilizing Technology Tools

1. Task Management Apps: Leverage task management apps to create to-do lists, set

reminders, and track progress. Apps like Todoist, Asana, or Trello can be particularly useful in organizing tasks and ensuring nothing falls through the cracks.

2. Calendar Alerts: Set calendar alerts and reminders for important deadlines and meetings. Regular notifications can serve as prompts and help individuals with ADHD stay on track with their schedules.

3. Focus Apps: Use apps designed to enhance focus and minimize distractions. Tools like Forest or Focus@Will can help maintain concentration by blocking out unnecessary stimuli during work sessions.

**Creating an Organized Workspace**

1. Declutter Regularly: A clutter-free workspace is essential for maintaining focus. Schedule regular

decluttering sessions to keep the workspace organized and reduce visual distractions.

2. Use Organization Tools: Implement organizational tools such as file folders, labels, and storage containers to keep materials easily accessible. A well-organized workspace contributes to a more efficient workflow.

3. Single-Tasking Zones: Designate specific areas for focused, single-tasking work. Creating zones where multitasking is discouraged can help individuals with ADHD concentrate on one task at a time.

Seeking Accountability and Support

1. Accountability Partners: Pairing up with an accountability partner can provide motivation and support. Discuss goals and deadlines with a trusted colleague or friend who can offer encouragement and check in on progress.

2. Professional Support: Seek professional support from mentors, coaches, or counselors who specialize in ADHD. These individuals can provide tailored guidance and strategies for overcoming specific challenges in the workplace.

3. Team Accountability: Establish team accountability mechanisms where members regularly check in on each other's progress. This can create a supportive environment where everyone is working collectively towards shared goals.

Reflecting and Adjusting

1. Regular Reflection: Schedule regular reflection periods to assess time management strategies. Identify what is working well and where adjustments can be made. This ongoing evaluation allows for continuous improvement.

2. Adjusting Strategies: Recognize that what works for one individual may not work for another. Be open to adjusting strategies based on personal preferences and evolving needs. Flexibility is key in finding the most effective approach.

3. Celebrate Achievements: Celebrate both small and large achievements. Recognizing accomplishments, even those that may seem minor, boosts motivation and reinforces positive habits.

Ultimately, the major thing here is to accept a combination of techniques that work best for individual preferences and needs. Time management is a skill that can be developed and refined over time, leading to increased confidence, reduced stress, and greater success in the professional realm. Through a commitment to continuous improvement and a willingness to explore and adapt various strategies, individuals with ADHD can navigate their professional responsibilities with greater ease and efficiency.

# Chapter 5

## Communication Skills and Neurodiversity

Enhancing Interpersonal Communication for Individuals with ADHD and Promoting Understanding Among Coworkers

Effective communication is at the heart of successful professional relationships. For individuals with ADHD, who may encounter challenges related to attention, focus, and social interactions, developing strong communication skills is crucial. For this reason, this chapter will analyze strategies to enhance interpersonal communication for individuals with ADHD and promote a culture of understanding and inclusion among coworkers.

Understanding ADHD and Communication Challenges

## Social and Communication Impacts

ADHD can influence various aspects of social interaction and communication. Individuals with ADHD may experience difficulties in maintaining attention during conversations, impulsivity in speech, and challenges in interpreting non-verbal cues. These factors can contribute to misunderstandings and affect relationships in the workplace.

## Hyperfocus and Distraction

The tendency to hyperfocus on specific tasks or topics can lead to challenges in shifting attention during conversations. On the other hand, distractions, both internal and external, may interrupt the flow of communication for individuals with ADHD. Understanding these dynamics is crucial for improving communication strategies.

## Impulsivity and Filtered Speech

Impulsivity in speech, a common trait in ADHD, can result in unfiltered comments or interruptions during conversations. Individuals with ADHD may struggle with the executive function of self-monitoring, leading to occasional bluntness or difficulty in gauging social cues.

## Effective Communication Strategies for Individuals with ADHD

### Active Listening Techniques

1. Maintain Eye Contact: Cultivate the habit of maintaining appropriate eye contact during conversations. This not only signals engagement but also helps individuals with ADHD stay focused on the speaker.

2. Reflective Listening: Practice reflective listening by paraphrasing or summarizing what the speaker has said. This technique ensures that the individual with ADHD processes information more thoroughly and clarifies any potential misunderstandings.

3. Ask Clarifying Questions: Encourage individuals with ADHD to ask clarifying questions when needed. Seeking additional information helps in maintaining a clear understanding of the conversation and demonstrates active engagement.

Communication Pacing

1. Use Pauses: Incorporate intentional pauses during conversations. This allows individuals with ADHD to process information, formulate responses, and avoid the impulsivity associated with rapid speech.

2. Signal Transitions: Signal transitions in conversation clearly. Providing a brief overview or summary before changing topics helps individuals with ADHD navigate shifts in focus more smoothly.

3. Provide Written Summaries: In situations where detailed information is shared verbally, provide a written summary afterward. This additional reference allows individuals with ADHD to review and reinforce their understanding.

Executive Function Support

1. Time Management: Integrate time management techniques into communication. Use visual aids, calendars, or reminders to help individuals with ADHD stay on track with meetings, deadlines, and other time-sensitive tasks.

2. Task Prioritization: Assist in task prioritization by clearly outlining the importance and urgency of different responsibilities. Breaking down larger

projects into smaller, manageable tasks can make prioritization more manageable.

3. Structured Communication: Introduce structured communication formats for important information. This may include agendas for meetings, written instructions, or organized presentations, providing a clear framework for information dissemination.

Self-Advocacy and Communication Preferences

1. Open Communication: Encourage open communication about individual preferences and needs. Individuals with ADHD should feel empowered to communicate their preferred communication styles, whether it involves written communication, face-to-face interactions, or a combination of both.

2. Use of Technology: Leverage technology to support communication preferences. For example, email or messaging platforms may be more

comfortable for individuals with ADHD, allowing for more thoughtful and structured responses.

3. Provide Feedback Opportunities: Establish regular feedback sessions to allow individuals with ADHD to express their experiences and provide insights into communication effectiveness. This two-way communication ensures continuous improvement.

## Promoting Understanding Among Coworkers

### Neurodiversity Training

1. Organize Workshops: Host neurodiversity workshops to educate coworkers about ADHD and other neurodivergent conditions. These workshops create awareness, dispel myths, and foster a culture of understanding and acceptance.

2. Include Personal Experiences: Personal stories and experiences from individuals with ADHD can be powerful tools for building empathy. Incorporate these narratives into training sessions to provide firsthand perspectives on challenges and strengths.

3. Discuss Communication Styles: Address different communication styles within the team. Highlight the diversity in approaches to processing information and encourage coworkers to adapt their communication methods when necessary.

Building a Supportive Environment

1. Establish a Support Network: Create a support network within the workplace where individuals with ADHD can connect with colleagues who understand their neurodivergent experiences. This network can offer guidance, share coping strategies, and provide a sense of community.

2. Promote Flexibility: Encourage flexibility in work arrangements to accommodate the unique needs of individuals with ADHD. Flexible schedules, remote work options, and personalized workspaces contribute to a more supportive and inclusive environment.

3. Mental Health Initiatives: Integrate mental health initiatives into the workplace to support overall well-being. This includes access to counseling services, stress management resources, and a culture that prioritizes mental health.

Facilitating Inclusive Meetings

1. Provide Agendas in Advance: Distribute meeting agendas in advance, allowing individuals with ADHD to prepare and organize their thoughts. This proactive approach contributes to more effective and focused meetings.

2. Designate Speaking Turns: Implement designated speaking turns during meetings. This structure ensures that everyone has an opportunity to contribute without feeling overwhelmed by the dynamics of group discussions.

3. Utilize Visual Aids: Enhance meetings with visual aids, such as charts or slides. Visual information can aid individuals with ADHD in processing and retaining information, making meetings more accessible and productive.

Conflict Resolution and Collaboration

Conflict Resolution Strategies

1. Structured Problem-Solving: Encourage structured problem-solving approaches during conflicts. Clearly define the issue, consider alternative solutions, and collaboratively choose the

most effective resolution. This methodical process minimizes impulsivity in decision-making.

2. Mediation Support: Provide mediation support when conflicts arise. Mediators can help individuals with ADHD and their colleagues navigate discussions, ensuring that perspectives are heard and resolutions are reached collaboratively.

Collaboration Techniques

1. Team-building Activities: Engage in team-building activities that promote understanding and collaboration. These activities foster a positive team culture and encourage colleagues to appreciate each other's strengths and differences.

2. Cross-training Opportunities: Implement cross-training opportunities where team members learn about each other's roles and responsibilities.

This mutual understanding promotes a more cohesive and supportive working environment.

3. Diverse Perspectives: Embrace diverse perspectives within the team. Recognize that individuals with ADHD may bring unique insights and approaches to problem-solving, contributing to a more innovative and dynamic team.

Continuous Learning and Improvement

Ongoing Education and Feedback

1. Regular Training Sessions: Conduct regular training sessions on communication skills, neurodiversity, and related topics. Ongoing education ensures that coworkers remain informed and continue to develop their understanding of neurodivergent experiences.

2. Feedback Loops: Establish feedback loops to gather insights from individuals with ADHD and their coworkers. This continuous feedback process allows for adjustments to communication strategies and ensures that the workplace remains responsive to evolving needs.

Professional Development Opportunities

1. Skill-building Workshops: Offer skill-building workshops focused on communication and interpersonal skills. These workshops provide practical tools and strategies that benefit all employees, fostering a culture of continuous improvement.

2. Coaching and Mentorship: Provide coaching and mentorship opportunities for individuals with ADHD. This personalized support helps individuals navigate their professional development journey,

enhancing both their communication skills and overall effectiveness in the workplace.

# Chapter 6

## Accepting Neurodiversity: Shaping Company Culture

# How Companies Can Create an Environment that Celebrates Neurodiversity and Encourages the Unique Contributions of Individuals with ADHD

## Introduction

Accepting neurodiversity is not just a moral imperative; it is a strategic decision that can transform company cultures, drive innovation, and enhance overall organizational success. In this chapter, we delve into the significance of neurodiversity in the workplace, exploring how companies can cultivate an environment that celebrates the unique contributions of individuals with ADHD. From fostering inclusion to reimagining recruitment processes, organizations play a pivotal role in shaping a company culture that values and harnesses the strengths of neurodivergent individuals.

## The Business Case for Neurodiversity

Driving Innovation

1. Diverse Perspectives: Neurodivergent individuals, including those with ADHD, often possess unique perspectives and approaches to problem-solving. Embracing neurodiversity in the workplace cultivates an environment where a range of creative solutions can emerge, driving innovation and enhancing the company's competitive edge.

2. Out-of-the-Box Thinking: The cognitive diversity that neurodivergent individuals bring can lead to out-of-the-box thinking. This fresh approach to challenges can break through conventional barriers, fostering a culture of innovation and adaptability.

Improving Problem-Solving

1. Analytical Skills: Many individuals with ADHD exhibit strong analytical and problem-solving skills. These skills, when harnessed effectively, contribute to more robust decision-making processes within the organization.

2. Hyperfocus Advantages: The hyperfocus characteristic of ADHD can be leveraged as a strength. In situations where intense concentration on a specific task is required, individuals with ADHD can excel, providing valuable contributions to complex projects.

Enhancing Workplace Dynamics

1. Team Dynamics: Neurodiversity enriches team dynamics by bringing a variety of communication styles, working preferences, and problem-solving approaches. This diversity contributes to a more vibrant and dynamic workplace.

2. Employee Engagement: Employees are more engaged and motivated when they feel valued and included. Creating a neurodiverse-friendly environment fosters a sense of belonging, leading to higher job satisfaction and increased productivity.

**Creating an Inclusive Recruitment Process**

Neurodiversity Hiring Programs

1. Targeted Recruitment Initiatives: Develop targeted recruitment initiatives specifically aimed at neurodivergent individuals. These programs can include partnerships with neurodiversity-focused organizations, participation in job fairs, and targeted outreach to educational institutions.

2. Neurodiversity-Friendly Job Descriptions: Craft job descriptions that are neurodiversity-friendly.

Use clear language, avoid jargon, and focus on the essential skills and qualifications required for the position. This approach attracts a broader pool of candidates.

Inclusive Interview Processes

1. Flexible Interview Formats  Offer flexibility in interview formats. Some neurodivergent individuals may perform better in non-traditional interview settings. Providing options such as skills assessments, project-based interviews, or video submissions allows candidates to showcase their abilities in a more comfortable environment.

2. Neurodiversity Training for Interviewers: Train interviewers on neurodiversity awareness and best practices. This education equips interviewers to recognize and appreciate diverse communication styles, providing a more inclusive and accommodating interview experience.

## Creating Neurodiverse-Friendly Workspaces

### Flexible Work Arrangements

1. Remote Work Opportunities: Embrace remote work options to accommodate different working styles. For some individuals with ADHD, a flexible environment can enhance focus and productivity. Remote work opportunities contribute to a more inclusive and neurodiverse-friendly workspace.

2. Flexible Schedules: Implement flexible work schedules that allow employees to adapt their work hours to their natural energy and focus peaks. This flexibility contributes to a healthier work-life balance for neurodivergent individuals.

### Sensory Considerations

1. Quiet Spaces: Designate quiet workspaces for individuals who may be sensitive to noise. Providing areas where employees can retreat for focused, uninterrupted work supports the sensory needs of neurodivergent individuals.

2. Personalization of Workstations: Encourage the personalization of workstations. Allowing individuals to customize their workspace based on their preferences fosters a sense of comfort and ownership, contributing to overall well-being.

Supportive Technology

1. Assistive Technologies: Integrate assistive technologies into the workplace. Tools such as noise-cancelling headphones, task management apps, and other assistive devices can enhance the work experience for neurodivergent individuals.

2. Training on Technology Usage: Provide training on the effective use of technology. For

neurodivergent individuals, understanding and utilizing the right tools can significantly improve productivity and efficiency.

## Raising Neurodiversity Awareness

### Neurodiversity Training Programs

1. Workplace Workshops: Conduct neurodiversity workshops for all employees. These workshops can cover various neurodivergent conditions, including ADHD, and provide insights into how to foster an inclusive and supportive workplace culture.

2. Educational Materials: Distribute educational materials that highlight the strengths and challenges associated with neurodivergent conditions. This can be done through newsletters, internal communications, or dedicated sections on company intranets.

Employee Resource Groups (ERGs)

1. Establish Neurodiversity ERGs: Create Employee Resource Groups (ERGs) focused on neurodiversity. These groups provide a platform for neurodivergent individuals to connect, share experiences, and contribute to the development of neurodiversity initiatives within the company.

2. Networking Events: Organize networking events that bring together neurodivergent individuals, allies, and members of the broader workforce. These events create opportunities for informal interactions and help build a sense of community.

Leadership Involvement

1. Leadership Commitment: Ensure that leadership is actively committed to neurodiversity initiatives. Leadership involvement sends a powerful message

about the organization's values and fosters a culture where everyone feels included and valued.

2. Visibility of Neurodivergent Leaders: Increase the visibility of neurodivergent leaders within the organization. This representation at leadership levels not only provides role models for neurodivergent employees but also demonstrates the organization's commitment to diversity.

Implementing Accommodation Policies

Clear Communication

1. Transparency in Policies: Clearly communicate accommodation policies to all employees. Transparency helps reduce stigma and ensures that neurodivergent individuals feel comfortable requesting accommodations when needed.

2. Accessible Resources: Provide accessible resources detailing available accommodations. This information can be made available through company handbooks, online portals, or designated human resources representatives.

Flexibility in Work Practices

1. Job Flexibility: Offer job flexibility to accommodate individual needs. This may include modified work hours, personalized workstations, or task adjustments. Tailoring work practices to the strengths and challenges of neurodivergent individuals contributes to a more inclusive workplace.

2. Ongoing Communication: Maintain open and ongoing communication with neurodivergent employees about their accommodation needs. Regular check-ins ensure that accommodations remain effective and can be adjusted as needed.

Celebrating Neurodiversity Success Stories

Employee Spotlights

1. Highlighting Achievements: Spotlight neurodivergent employees and their achievements. This recognition not only celebrates individual successes but also demonstrates the value that neurodiversity brings to the organization.

2. Inclusion in Internal Communications: Incorporate neurodiversity success stories into internal communications. This could include newsletters, company-wide emails, or intranet features that showcase the diverse talents and accomplishments of neurodivergent individuals.

Recognition Programs

1. Neurodiversity Awards: Establish awards or recognition programs specifically focused on neurodiversity. Recognizing individuals, teams, or initiatives that contribute to a more inclusive and neurodiverse-friendly workplace reinforces the organization's commitment to diversity.

2. Inclusive Events: Integrate neurodiversity into company-wide events and celebrations. Whether it's during diversity and inclusion months or annual celebrations, incorporating neurodiversity highlights the organization's dedication to creating an inclusive environment.

Evaluating and Adapting Neurodiversity Initiatives

Data Collection and Analysis

1. Anonymous Surveys: Implement anonymous surveys to gather feedback on neurodiversity

initiatives. This feedback provides valuable insights into the effectiveness of existing programs and areas for improvement.

2. Regular Evaluation: Establish a regular evaluation process for neurodiversity initiatives. This ongoing assessment ensures that the organization remains responsive to the evolving needs of neurodivergent employees.

Continuous Improvement

1. Adaptation of Initiatives: Be willing to adapt neurodiversity initiatives based on feedback and evolving best practices. The ability to iterate and improve demonstrates the organization's commitment to creating a workplace that is truly inclusive.

2. Engage Neurodivergent Employees: Actively engage neurodivergent employees in the evaluation and improvement process. Their insights are

invaluable in shaping initiatives that genuinely address the unique needs of the neurodivergent community.

Thus, acknowledging neurodiversity is not a one-time initiative; it is an ongoing commitment to creating a workplace where every individual, regardless of neurodivergent status, feels valued, supported, and included. From recruitment practices to workspace design, communication strategies to recognition programs, fostering a neurodiverse-friendly company culture requires a holistic and sustained effort.

As organizations increasingly recognize the business benefits of neurodiversity, the journey toward inclusivity becomes a shared endeavor.

# Chapter 7

**Advocacy and Self-Advocacy in the Workplace**

Empowering Individuals with ADHD to Advocate for Themselves and Educating Employers on the Importance of Neurodiversity Inclusion

Advocacy and self-advocacy have important roles in creating a workplace that embraces neurodiversity, particularly for individuals with ADHD. In this chapter, thus, we will examine the significance of advocacy in the professional realm, examining how empowering individuals with ADHD to advocate for themselves contributes to a more inclusive workplace. Additionally, we delve into the crucial role employers play in understanding and championing neurodiversity, creating environments where diverse talents can flourish.

The Power of Advocacy

Advocacy involves actively supporting and promoting a cause, and in the context of the workplace, it means championing the rights, needs, and contributions of individuals with ADHD. Advocacy is a two-fold process that includes self-advocacy, where individuals with ADHD assert their needs and strengths, and external advocacy, where allies and organizations champion the cause of neurodiversity inclusion.

Impact on Workplace Culture

1. Fostering Inclusivity: Advocacy contributes to the creation of an inclusive culture. When individuals with ADHD feel empowered to express their needs and when employers actively support neurodiversity, it creates a workplace where everyone is valued for their unique contributions.

2. Breaking Stigmas: Advocacy helps break down stigmas associated with ADHD. By openly discussing neurodivergent experiences, individuals challenge misconceptions, fostering a more informed and understanding work environment.

Self-Advocacy for Individuals with ADHD

Understanding Individual Needs

1. Self-Reflection: Encourage individuals with ADHD to engage in self-reflection. Understanding personal strengths, challenges, and preferences is a crucial first step in effective self-advocacy.

2. Communication Styles: Identify preferred communication styles. Some individuals may find written communication more comfortable, while others may prefer face-to-face interactions. Recognizing these preferences aids in effective self-expression.

Articulating Needs and Accommodations

1. Clear Communication: Emphasize the importance of clear communication when expressing needs. Clearly articulating how ADHD manifests for each individual helps colleagues and supervisors understand how to offer support.

2. Educating Others: Actively engage in educating colleagues and supervisors about ADHD. Provide resources, share personal experiences, and emphasize the importance of neurodiversity in the workplace.

Establishing Boundaries

1. Identifying Triggers: Work on identifying triggers that may impact focus or well-being. Communicate these triggers to colleagues to establish understanding and support.

2. Negotiating Work Arrangements: Where possible, negotiate work arrangements that accommodate individual needs. This might include

flexible work hours, quiet spaces, or specific tools and technologies.

## External Advocacy for Neurodiversity Inclusion

### Employer Education

1. Workplace Training Programs: Advocate for workplace training programs on neurodiversity. Encourage employers to invest in educating staff at all levels about the unique strengths and challenges associated with ADHD and other neurodivergent conditions.

2. Expert Consultations: Facilitate expert consultations within the organization. Bringing in specialists who can provide insights on neurodiversity helps dispel myths and fosters a culture of informed understanding.

Establishing Neurodiversity Policies

1. Inclusive Policies: Advocate for the development of inclusive policies that explicitly address neurodiversity. These policies should encompass recruitment, hiring, accommodations, and ongoing support for neurodivergent employees.

2. Transparent Communication: Encourage transparent communication regarding neurodiversity initiatives. Regularly update employees on the organization's commitment to neurodiversity inclusion and the progress made in implementing related policies.

Building Neurodiverse-Friendly Workspaces

Workspace Design and Accommodations

1. Sensory Considerations: Advocate for sensory considerations in workspace design. This might

involve creating quiet areas, providing noise-cancelling headphones, or allowing for personalized workstations.

2. Flexible Work Arrangements: Promote flexible work arrangements that accommodate the diverse needs of neurodivergent individuals. This includes options for remote work, flexible schedules, and personalized work environments.

Mental Health Initiatives

1. Access to Support Services: Advocate for increased access to mental health support services. Ensure that employees, including those with ADHD, have resources such as counseling and stress management programs.

2. Promotion of Well-being: Encourage initiatives that promote overall well-being, recognizing the connection between mental health and productivity. Activities such as mindfulness

sessions or wellness programs contribute to a supportive workplace culture.

## Navigating Disclosure and Privacy

### Personal Decision-Making

1. Informed Decision: Empower individuals with ADHD to make informed decisions about disclosure. Discuss the potential benefits and risks associated with disclosing neurodivergent status in the workplace.

2. Educating Colleagues: For those who choose to disclose, provide guidance on how to educate colleagues and supervisors about ADHD. This might involve sharing educational resources, participating in awareness campaigns, or organizing workshops.

Privacy Protection

1. Confidentiality Policies: Advocate for confidentiality policies that protect the privacy of neurodivergent individuals. Ensure that personal information related to ADHD is handled with sensitivity and respect.

2. Addressing Stigma: Work toward creating an environment where disclosure is met with understanding rather than judgment. Addressing stigma through education and awareness initiatives helps foster a more accepting workplace.

Legal Protections and Rights

Understanding Legal Frameworks

1. Legal Protections: Advocate for awareness of legal protections and rights for neurodivergent individuals. Ensure that employees are informed

about laws and regulations that safeguard against discrimination based on neurodivergent status.

2. Anti-Discrimination Policies: Work toward the development and reinforcement of anti-discrimination policies that explicitly include neurodiversity. This ensures that neurodivergent individuals are protected against discriminatory practices.

Accessibility Accommodations

1. Accessible Work Environments: Advocate for accessible work environments. This includes physical accessibility as well as accommodations such as assistive technologies or modified work arrangements.

2. Training on Accommodations: Provide training to employees and supervisors on the implementation of accommodations. Awareness and understanding of how accommodations work

contribute to a smoother integration of neurodivergent individuals into the workplace.

Collaborative Initiatives

Employee Resource Groups (ERGs)

1. Establish Neurodiversity ERGs: Advocate for the creation of Neurodiversity Employee Resource Groups (ERGs). These groups provide a platform for mutual support, shared experiences, and collective advocacy within the organization.

2. Collaboration Across ERGs: Encourage collaboration between neurodiversity ERGs and other diversity-focused ERGs. Building alliances across different groups contributes to a more comprehensive and inclusive approach to workplace diversity.

Collaborative Projects

1. Participate in Collaborative Projects: Advocate for participation in collaborative projects that promote neurodiversity inclusion. This might involve partnerships with external organizations, joint initiatives with other companies, or involvement in industry-wide neurodiversity awareness campaigns.

2. Engage in Industry Advocacy: Actively engage in advocacy efforts within the broader industry. By participating in discussions, conferences, and collaborative projects, organizations can contribute to the advancement of neurodiversity inclusion on a larger scale.

Employee Training Programs

Ongoing Education

1. Regular Training Sessions: Advocate for regular training sessions on neurodiversity for all employees. Continuous education ensures that awareness remains high, reducing the likelihood of stereotypes and biases.

2. Interactive Workshops: Incorporate interactive workshops that facilitate understanding and empathy. Engaging employees in activities that simulate neurodivergent experiences fosters a deeper appreciation for the challenges faced by individuals with ADHD.

Inclusive Leadership Training

1. Leadership Involvement: Advocate for the inclusion of neurodiversity in leadership training programs. Ensure that leaders understand the importance of fostering an inclusive culture and are

equipped to support neurodivergent individuals within their teams.

2. Inclusive Leadership Practices: Provide guidance on inclusive leadership practices. This may involve incorporating neurodiversity considerations into performance evaluations, mentorship programs, and leadership development initiatives.

In conclusion, advocacy and self-advocacy are powerful catalysts for change in the workplace. As we move forward, it is not just a commitment to compliance with legal standards but a commitment to creating workplaces that genuinely value the richness that neurodiversity brings to the professional landscape. In advocating for neurodiversity, we not only transform individual lives but also contribute to a collective shift toward a more inclusive and innovative future of work.

# Chapter 8

**Thriving in Teamwork: Collaboration Strategies for ADHD Professionals**

Tips for Effective Collaboration and Teamwork, Emphasizing the Strengths that Individuals with ADHD Bring to Group Projects

Thriving in teamwork is a critical aspect of professional success, and individuals with ADHD possess unique strengths that can significantly contribute to collaborative efforts. In this chapter, we explore effective collaboration and teamwork strategies tailored to the strengths of individuals with ADHD. From leveraging creativity to navigating potential challenges, we'll provide insights and practical tips for fostering an inclusive and productive team environment.

**Understanding the Strengths of Individuals with ADHD in Teamwork**

Creativity and Innovation

1. Divergent Thinking: Individuals with ADHD often exhibit divergent thinking, generating a wide array of ideas. Embrace this creativity within team projects by encouraging brainstorming sessions where all ideas are welcomed.

2. Adaptability: The ability to quickly shift focus, known as hyperfocus, can be harnessed as a strength. Individuals with ADHD may bring adaptability to the team, responding effectively to changing project requirements and timelines.

Hyperfocus and Specialization

1. Deep Dives into Tasks: Leverage hyperfocus for tasks that require intense concentration. Assigning specific responsibilities that align with an individual's interests can lead to exceptional results in their specialized areas.

2. Niche Expertise: Recognize and appreciate the niche expertise that individuals with ADHD may

develop. Their hyperfocus allows them to delve deeply into subjects, contributing valuable insights to the team.

Energetic and Enthusiastic Approach

1. Elevating Team Morale: Individuals with ADHD often bring enthusiasm and energy to the team. Channel this positivity to boost team morale, especially during challenging phases of a project.

2. Infectious Passion: Their infectious passion for projects can inspire the team. This enthusiasm can be a driving force behind overcoming obstacles and fostering a collaborative spirit.

Effective Collaboration Strategies

Clear Communication

1.    Structured    Communication:    Implement structured communication to ensure clarity. This can include setting agendas for meetings, using concise and explicit language in written communication, and providing clear project guidelines.

2. Active Listening Techniques: Emphasize active listening within the team. Encourage individuals with ADHD to repeat or summarize key points to enhance their understanding, and promote a culture where everyone's input is valued.


Collaborative Tools and Technologies


1. Project Management Platforms: Integrate project management platforms to enhance organization and collaboration. Tools that provide clear task assignments, deadlines, and progress tracking can

help individuals with ADHD stay on top of their responsibilities.

2. Communication Apps: Leverage communication apps for real-time collaboration. Instant messaging platforms can facilitate quick exchanges, allowing team members to stay connected and address questions efficiently.

Task Delegation and Role Clarity

1. Clearly Defined Roles: Establish clearly defined roles within the team. Clearly outlining responsibilities helps individuals with ADHD understand their contributions and fosters a sense of accountability.

2. Task Delegation Meetings: Conduct task delegation meetings where roles and expectations are communicated. Providing a dedicated space for clarifying assignments ensures that everyone is on the same page.

Time Management Techniques

1. Visual Timelines: Use visual timelines to illustrate project milestones. Visual aids, such as Gantt charts or timelines, can help individuals with ADHD grasp the project's overall timeline and better manage their time.

2. Prioritization Strategies: Assist in task prioritization by helping individuals identify key priorities. Breaking down larger tasks into smaller, manageable steps can make it easier for team members with ADHD to navigate their responsibilities.

Inclusive Meeting Practices

1. Structured Meetings: Conduct structured meetings with clear agendas. This helps individuals with ADHD anticipate discussion topics and

mentally prepare, contributing to more focused and productive meetings.

2. Designated Speaking Turns: Implement designated speaking turns during meetings. This practice ensures that everyone has an opportunity to contribute, minimizing potential challenges related to impulsivity in communication.

Flexibility in Work Arrangements

1. Flexible Work Hours: Embrace flexible work hours to accommodate individual needs. Allowing individuals with ADHD to work during their peak focus times can enhance their productivity and overall contribution to the team.

2. Remote Work Options: Provide remote work options when feasible. Some individuals with ADHD may find a personalized, distraction-free environment conducive to optimal performance.

Encouraging Open Feedback

1. Constructive Feedback Culture: Foster a culture of constructive feedback. Encourage team members, including those with ADHD, to provide and receive feedback openly, promoting continuous improvement within the team.

2. Regular Check-ins: Conduct regular check-ins to discuss progress, challenges, and goals. These check-ins create a supportive environment where individuals with ADHD can express their needs and receive guidance.

Navigating Challenges in Teamwork

Addressing Potential Misunderstandings

1. Communication Clarity: Emphasize the importance of clear and explicit communication to minimize misunderstandings. Encourage team members to seek clarification when needed and to express themselves in a way that ensures their message is understood.

2. Building Communication Skills: Provide opportunities for building communication skills. Workshops or training sessions focused on effective communication can benefit the entire team, fostering a more harmonious and understanding work environment.

Impulsivity in Decision-Making

1. Structured Decision-Making Processes: Implement structured decision-making processes. By establishing clear steps for decision-making, teams can mitigate the potential challenges

associated with impulsivity and ensure that decisions are well-considered.

2. Pause and Reflect Techniques: Encourage the use of pause-and-reflect techniques. Individuals with ADHD can benefit from incorporating brief pauses before responding, allowing them to gather their thoughts and respond thoughtfully.

Managing Time Constraints

1. Effective Time Management Training: Provide effective time management training. Workshops or resources that offer practical strategies for managing time, setting priorities, and meeting deadlines can be particularly beneficial for individuals with ADHD.

2. Adapting to Individual Work Styles: Recognize and adapt to individual work styles within the team. Understanding the diverse ways in which team members approach tasks and deadlines contributes

to a more flexible and accommodating work environment.

Conflict Resolution Strategies

1. Mediation Support: Offer mediation support when conflicts arise. Mediators can help facilitate discussions, ensuring that all perspectives are heard and guiding the team toward collaborative resolutions.

2. Structured Problem-Solving: Encourage structured problem-solving approaches. Clearly defining the issue, considering alternative solutions, and collaboratively choosing the most effective resolution can minimize conflicts within the team.

Celebrating Team Success

Recognizing Individual Contributions

1. Individual Acknowledgments: Acknowledge individual contributions within the team. Recognizing the unique strengths and accomplishments of each team member, including those with ADHD, fosters a sense of pride and motivation.

2. Team Celebrations: Celebrate team successes collectively. Establish a culture of appreciation where milestones, achievements, and successful project completions are recognized and celebrated as a team.

Employee Appreciation Initiatives

1. Employee Recognition Programs: Advocate for employee recognition programs that highlight exceptional contributions. These programs can include awards, certificates, or other forms of recognition that showcase the diverse talents within the team.

2. Public Acknowledgment: Encourage public acknowledgment of achievements. Whether through internal communications, company-wide meetings, or social media, publicly recognizing team accomplishments reinforces the value of each team member's efforts.

Thriving in teamwork requires a blend of effective communication, understanding of individual strengths, and collaborative strategies that accommodate diverse working styles. For individuals with ADHD, recognizing and embracing their unique contributions can lead to more innovative and successful team outcomes.

# Chapter 9

**Overcoming Workplace Challenges: ADHD and Stress Management**

Coping Mechanisms and Stress Management Strategies Tailored to the Specific Needs of Individuals with ADHD in a Professional Context

Navigating the complexities of the workplace can be challenging for individuals with ADHD, and managing stress is a crucial aspect of maintaining well-being and performance. In this chapter, we will delve into the unique challenges that individuals with ADHD may face in professional settings and explore tailored coping mechanisms and stress management strategies.

Understanding ADHD and Workplace Stress

Identifying Workplace Stressors

1. Task Overload: Individuals with ADHD may struggle with managing multiple tasks

simultaneously. Recognizing the signs of task overload and developing strategies to prioritize and organize work can mitigate stress.

2. Time Pressure: Time constraints can be particularly stressful for individuals with ADHD. Implementing effective time management techniques and setting realistic deadlines can help alleviate this pressure.

Sensory Sensitivities

1. Open Workspaces: Open office environments, common in many workplaces, can be overwhelming for individuals with ADHD due to sensory sensitivities. Creating designated quiet spaces or providing noise-canceling headphones can offer relief.

2. Visual Distractions: Minimizing visual distractions, such as excessive decorations or

clutter, can create a more focused and comfortable workspace for individuals with ADHD.

Executive Function Challenges

1. Organization Difficulties: Challenges in organization and planning are common for individuals with ADHD. Implementing organizational tools, such as calendars and task lists, can provide structure and reduce stress.

2. Memory Issues: Forgetfulness and memory issues can contribute to workplace stress. Encouraging the use of reminders, notes, and digital tools can support individuals in remembering important tasks and deadlines.

Tailored Coping Mechanisms for ADHD Professionals

Breaks and Movement

1. Frequent Breaks: Advocate for and schedule frequent breaks throughout the day. Short breaks can help individuals with ADHD recharge and maintain focus.

2. Physical Activity: Encourage regular physical activity. Exercise has been shown to positively impact attention and mood, making it a valuable tool for managing stress.

Mindfulness and Relaxation Techniques

1. Mindfulness Practices: Introduce mindfulness practices into the workplace. Techniques such as deep breathing, meditation, or guided imagery can help individuals with ADHD center themselves and manage stress.

2. Scheduled Relaxation Time: Promote the scheduling of relaxation time. Creating designated

periods for relaxation, even if brief, allows individuals to decompress and refocus.

## Clear Communication Strategies

1. Structured Communication: Emphasize the importance of structured communication. Clear and concise communication helps individuals with ADHD better understand expectations, reducing ambiguity and stress.

2. Regular Check-Ins: Implement regular check-ins with supervisors or team members. These meetings provide opportunities to discuss progress, address concerns, and ensure that individuals feel supported.

## Task Modification and Simplification

1. Breaking Down Tasks: Encourage breaking down complex tasks into smaller, manageable steps. This

approach helps individuals with ADHD approach work in a more organized and less overwhelming manner.

2. Simplified Instructions: Provide simplified instructions. Clear and straightforward guidance supports understanding and execution, minimizing potential stressors related to task complexity.

Workspace Personalization

1. Personalized Workstations: Allow for personalized workstations. Allowing individuals to organize their workspace according to their preferences can create a more comfortable and conducive environment.

2. Sensory Comfort Items: Permit the use of sensory comfort items. Fidget tools, stress balls, or other

sensory-friendly items can provide a discreet outlet for managing stress in the workplace.

Time Management Strategies

1. Visual Timelines: Implement visual timelines for projects. Visual aids, such as Gantt charts, provide a clear overview of project timelines, aiding individuals with ADHD in managing their time effectively.

2. Prioritization Techniques: Teach prioritization techniques. Supporting individuals in identifying and focusing on high-priority tasks can enhance their ability to manage time and reduce stress.

Emotional Regulation Support

1. Accessible Support Resources: Ensure access to emotional support resources. Providing information on available counseling services or Employee Assistance Programs (EAPs) can offer assistance in times of emotional distress.

2. Emotion Regulation Techniques: Educate individuals on emotion regulation techniques. Techniques such as cognitive-behavioral strategies or journaling can help manage and process emotions related to workplace stress.

Building a Supportive Workplace Environment

Inclusive Policies and Accommodations

1. Flexible Work Arrangements: Advocate for flexible work arrangements. Allowing individuals to tailor their work hours or work remotely when

needed accommodates the diverse needs of individuals with ADHD.

2. Accommodations for Sensory Needs: Implement accommodations for sensory needs. Providing options for individuals to modify their work environment based on sensory preferences contributes to a more comfortable workspace.

Training and Awareness Programs

1. Neurodiversity Training: Offer neurodiversity training programs. Training sessions that educate employees and supervisors about ADHD promote understanding and create a more inclusive workplace.

2. Stress Management Workshops: Conduct stress management workshops. Workshops tailored to the needs of individuals with ADHD can provide practical tools and strategies for navigating workplace stress.

Employee Assistance Programs (EAPs)

1. Accessible Resources: Promote awareness of Employee Assistance Programs (EAPs). Ensure that individuals are aware of available resources for seeking support in managing stress and other personal challenges.

2. Confidential Counseling Services: Offer confidential counseling services. Providing access to professional counseling can be a valuable resource for individuals dealing with workplace stress.

Peer Support Networks

1. Establish Peer Support Networks: Establish peer support networks within the organization. Peer mentors or support groups create a sense of

community and offer individuals the opportunity to share experiences and coping strategies.

2. Mentorship Programs: Implement mentorship programs. Pairing individuals with ADHD with mentors who have experience navigating similar challenges can provide guidance and support.

Encouraging Open Communication

Reducing Stigma

1. Stigma Reduction Initiatives: Advocate for stigma reduction initiatives. Openly discussing ADHD and promoting understanding can contribute to reducing stigma in the workplace.

2. Personal Testimonials: Encourage personal testimonials. Individuals sharing their experiences with ADHD can humanize the condition, fostering empathy and support from colleagues.

Inclusive Language

1. Promote Inclusive Language: Promote the use of inclusive language. Encouraging respectful and inclusive communication helps create a positive and supportive atmosphere for individuals with ADHD.

2. Education on Neurodiversity: Provide education on neurodiversity. Ensuring that employees understand the diversity of cognitive styles fosters an environment where individuals with ADHD feel accepted and valued.

Building Resilience for Long-Term Success

Goal Setting and Celebrating Achievements

1. SMART Goal Setting: Encourage SMART goal setting. Setting Specific, Measurable, Achievable, Relevant, and Time-bound goals helps individuals with ADHD stay focused and motivated.

2. Celebrating Milestones: Celebrate achievement, no matter how small. Acknowledging and celebrating milestones along the way contributes to a positive work experience and boosts morale.

Reflective Practices

1. Regular Reflection: Promote regular reflection on accomplishments and challenges. Encouraging individuals to reflect on their experiences helps build self-awareness and resilience.

2. Adaptability Skills: Foster adaptability skills. Individuals with ADHD can develop resilience by learning to adapt to changing circumstances and setbacks, cultivating a mindset of continuous learning.

Professional Development Opportunities

1. Tailored Training Programs: Implement tailored professional development programs. Offering training programs that address the specific needs of individuals with ADHD supports their growth and success in the workplace.

2. Skill Enhancement Workshops: Conduct skill enhancement workshops. Workshops focused on developing skills such as time management, organizational strategies, and effective communication contribute to long-term success.

Legal Protections and Advocacy

Understanding Legal Rights

1. Employee Rights Education: Educate individuals about their legal rights. Understanding legal protections against discrimination based on neurodivergent status empowers individuals to advocate for their rights.

2. Anti-Discrimination Policies: Advocate for strong anti-discrimination policies. Ensuring that organizational policies explicitly address neurodiversity helps create a workplace that values diversity and inclusion.

Advocacy Initiatives

1. Participation in Advocacy Efforts: Encourage participation in advocacy efforts. Individuals with ADHD can contribute to broader neurodiversity advocacy initiatives, fostering a sense of purpose and empowerment.

2. Collaboration with Neurodiversity Organizations: Collaborate with neurodiversity organizations. Building partnerships with external advocacy groups can enhance workplace support for individuals with ADHD.

# Chapter 10

## Professional Development and Career Growth

Guidance on Navigating Career Paths, Setting Realistic Goals, and Leveraging ADHD Traits for Personal and Professional Development

Here in this chapter, we will explore strategies tailored to help neurodivergent professionals navigate career paths, set realistic goals, and leverage the unique traits associated with ADHD for personal and professional development.

Navigating Career Paths with ADHD

Self-Exploration and Assessment

1. Identifying Strengths: Conduct a thorough self-assessment to identify personal strengths. Recognizing areas of proficiency allows individuals to align their career paths with activities that capitalize on their unique skills.

2. Passion Exploration: Explore personal passions and interests. Individuals with ADHD often thrive when engaged in activities they are passionate about, making it essential to align career choices with these intrinsic motivators.

Career Counseling and Mentorship

1. Seeking Professional Guidance: Consider seeking career counseling services. Professional guidance can provide insights into suitable career paths based on individual strengths, interests, and goals.

2. Mentorship Programs: Participate in mentorship programs. Mentors can offer valuable advice, share experiences, and provide guidance on navigating the complexities of a chosen career.

Skill Development Opportunities

1. Continuous Learning: Embrace a mindset of continuous learning. Taking advantage of skill development opportunities, such as workshops, courses, or certifications, ensures that individuals stay relevant in their chosen fields.

2. Networking Events: Attend networking events. Building a professional network opens doors to potential mentors, job opportunities, and valuable insights into different career paths.

Setting Realistic Career Goals

SMART Goal Setting

1. Specific Goals: Set specific and clearly defined goals. Individuals with ADHD benefit from goals that are Specific, Measurable, Achievable, Relevant, and Time-bound (SMART), providing a structured framework for success.

2. Break Down Goals: Break down larger goals into smaller, manageable steps. This approach facilitates progress tracking and helps avoid feeling overwhelmed by the magnitude of a goal.

Time Management Strategies

1. Effective Time Blocking: Implement effective time-blocking techniques. Breaking the day into focused time blocks for specific tasks enhances productivity and supports individuals in achieving their career goals.

2. Prioritization Methods: Develop prioritization methods. ADHD individuals may find it helpful to prioritize tasks based on urgency and importance, ensuring that crucial activities are addressed first.

Flexibility in Goal Adjustment

1. Adapting to Changing Circumstances: Cultivate adaptability in goal-setting. Being open to adjusting goals based on changing circumstances allows for a more realistic and resilient approach to career development.

2. Learning from Setbacks: View setbacks as learning opportunities. Individuals with ADHD may encounter challenges, but viewing setbacks positively and learning from them contributes to long-term growth.

Leveraging ADHD Traits for Success

Creativity and Innovation

1. Identifying Creative Outlets: Identify creative outlets within professional roles. ADHD individuals often possess a high degree of creativity; leveraging this trait in problem-solving and innovation can lead to unique contributions in the workplace.

2. Innovative Problem-Solving: Embrace innovative problem-solving approaches. ADHD individuals may excel at thinking outside the box, providing fresh perspectives and solutions to workplace challenges.

Hyperfocus and Specialization

1. Specializing in Niche Areas: Specialize in niche areas of interest. Hyperfocus, a common trait in ADHD, can be channeled into becoming an expert in specific subjects, enhancing career value.

2. Project Leadership: Take on project leadership roles. Individuals with ADHD may find that hyperfocus allows them to immerse themselves in projects, making them valuable contributors to leadership positions.

Energetic and Enthusiastic Approach

1. Motivating Team Members: Utilize energy and enthusiasm to motivate teams. Individuals with ADHD can bring contagious passion to projects, fostering a positive work environment and team morale.

2. Pitching Ideas Effectively: Leverage enthusiasm when pitching ideas. The ability to convey excitement about a project or initiative can be a powerful tool in gaining support from colleagues and superiors.

Overcoming Challenges in Professional Development

## Time Management Techniques

1. Time Management Workshops: Participate in time management workshops. Workshops specifically designed for individuals with ADHD can provide practical strategies for managing time effectively.

2. Time-Blocking Apps: Use time-blocking apps. Digital tools can assist in structuring the workday and allocating time to specific tasks, helping individuals stay organized and focused.

## Organizational Strategies

1. Implementing Organization Tools: Adopt organizational tools. Tools such as calendars, task management apps, and project management

software can assist individuals in maintaining organization and structure.

2. Creating Daily Checklists: Develop daily checklists. A checklist helps individuals prioritize tasks, track progress, and experience a sense of accomplishment at the end of each day.

Stress Management Techniques

1. Mindfulness Practices: Integrate mindfulness practices into the daily routine. Mindfulness can help individuals manage stress, improve focus, and enhance overall well-being.

2. Physical Exercise: Prioritize physical exercise. Regular exercise has been shown to reduce stress and improve cognitive function, making it a valuable tool for managing professional challenges.

Building a Support System

Peer Support Networks

1. Joining Professional Groups: Join professional groups or associations. These communities provide opportunities for networking, mentorship, and peer support, creating a sense of belonging.

2. Participating in Networking Events: Actively participate in networking events. Establishing connections with colleagues in similar career paths can offer valuable insights and support.

Communicating with Supervisors

1. Open Communication Channels: Maintain open communication with supervisors. Discussing career goals, challenges, and support needs ensures that supervisors are aware of individual aspirations and can provide appropriate guidance.

2. Requesting Feedback: Seek constructive feedback regularly. Proactively asking for feedback demonstrates a commitment to personal and professional growth and allows for continuous improvement.

Emotional Support Systems

1. Building Personal Support Systems: Cultivate personal support systems. Building strong connections with friends, family, or support groups outside of the workplace provides emotional resilience and encouragement.

2. Professional Counseling Services: Consider professional counseling services. Seeking guidance from a professional counselor can offer valuable insights and coping strategies for managing stress and challenges.

Career Transitions and Advancements

Pursuing Further Education

1. Identifying Learning Opportunities: Explore further education opportunities. Individuals with ADHD may benefit from additional certifications, courses, or degrees that align with their career goals.

2. Online Learning Platforms: Utilize online learning platforms. The flexibility of online courses accommodates various learning styles, allowing individuals to acquire new skills at their own pace.

Job Transitions

1. Exploring New Opportunities: Consider exploring new job opportunities. Job transitions

may provide fresh challenges, growth opportunities, and a chance to apply existing skills in different contexts.

2. Transferable Skills Assessment: Assess transferable skills. Identify skills acquired in current roles that are applicable to new opportunities, highlighting strengths in job applications and interviews.

Leadership Roles

1. Leadership Training Programs: Engage in leadership training programs. Developing leadership skills equips individuals with ADHD to take on more significant roles within their organizations.

2. Volunteering for Leadership Initiatives: Volunteer for leadership initiatives. Taking the initiative to lead projects or teams showcases

leadership potential and can lead to advancements in one's career.

## Advocacy for Neurodivergent Professionals

### Workplace Advocacy Initiatives

1. Participating in Advocacy Groups: Participate in neurodiversity advocacy groups. Joining or supporting organizations that promote neurodiversity fosters a sense of community and contributes to broader advocacy efforts.

2. Sharing Personal Experiences: Share personal experiences with ADHD. Opening up about one's journey can raise awareness, reduce stigma, and inspire others within the workplace.

### Mentorship and Support Programs

1. Initiating Mentorship Programs: Initiate or participate in mentorship programs. Supporting the growth of neurodivergent individuals through mentorship fosters a culture of inclusivity and professional development.

2. Providing Resources for Self-Advocacy: Equip individuals with resources for self-advocacy. Empowering neurodivergent professionals with information and tools to advocate for themselves contributes to a more supportive workplace.

# Chapter 11

## Legal Rights and Accommodations for ADHD in the Workplace

An Overview of Legal Rights and Accommodations Available to Individuals with ADHD, Ensuring Fair Treatment in the Professional Realm

Ensuring a fair and inclusive workplace for individuals with ADHD requires a comprehensive understanding of legal rights and the accommodations available to support their needs. In this chapter, we explore the legal framework surrounding ADHD in the workplace, providing an overview of the rights individuals hold and the accommodations that can be implemented to create an environment conducive to their success.

Understanding Legal Protections

Americans with Disabilities Act (ADA)

1. Overview of ADA: The Americans with Disabilities Act (ADA) is a key legislative framework providing protection against discrimination for individuals with disabilities, including ADHD. It prohibits discrimination in various aspects of employment, such as hiring, promotions, and termination, ensuring equal opportunities for individuals with ADHD.

2. Qualifying as a Disability: ADHD is considered a disability under the ADA. To qualify for protection, individuals must demonstrate that their condition substantially limits one or more major life

activities, such as learning, concentrating, or interacting with others.

Rehabilitation Act of 1973

1. Applicability to Federal Employers: The Rehabilitation Act of 1973 extends protections to federal employees. Section 501 prohibits discrimination against individuals with disabilities working in the federal government, requiring agencies to provide reasonable accommodations.

2. Reasonable Accommodations: Similar to the ADA, the Rehabilitation Act emphasizes the provision of reasonable accommodations. Federal agencies must make adjustments to the work environment or job tasks to ensure that individuals with disabilities, including ADHD, have an equal opportunity for employment and advancement.

State and Local Laws

1. Additional Protections: In addition to federal laws, various states and localities may have their own anti-discrimination laws providing additional protections for individuals with disabilities. Familiarizing oneself with the specific laws applicable in their location is crucial for understanding the full scope of legal rights.

2. Varied Definitions of Disability: State and local laws may define disability differently or provide additional categories of protection. Understanding the nuances of these laws is essential for individuals seeking legal recourse or accommodations.

Legal Rights for Individuals with ADHD

Protections Against Discrimination

1. Equal Employment Opportunity Commission (EEOC): The EEOC enforces federal laws prohibiting workplace discrimination. Individuals with ADHD can file complaints with the EEOC if they believe they have experienced discrimination based on their condition.

2. Protections During the Hiring Process: Employers are prohibited from discriminating against individuals with ADHD during the hiring process. Questions about an applicant's medical history, including ADHD, are generally not allowed until a job offer has been extended.

Confidentiality of Medical Information

1. Medical Privacy Rights: Employees with ADHD have the right to keep their medical information

private. Employers are generally not allowed to disclose an individual's ADHD diagnosis without their explicit consent.

2. Medical Examinations and Inquiries: Employers are restricted in their ability to conduct medical examinations or make disability-related inquiries. Any such actions must be job-related and consistent with business necessity.

Accommodations for ADHD in the Workplace

1. Reasonable Accommodations: Employers are required to provide reasonable accommodations to individuals with ADHD to ensure they can perform their job duties. These accommodations are intended to level the playing field and address the specific challenges associated with ADHD.

2. Examples of Reasonable Accommodations:

- Flexible work hours to accommodate peak focus times.

- Breaks to manage stress and maintain focus.

- Remote work options to create a distraction-free environment.

- Use of organizational tools such as calendars or task lists.

- Modification of workspace to reduce sensory distractions.

Requesting Accommodations and Disclosure

Disclosing ADHD to Employers

1. Voluntary Disclosure: Disclosing ADHD to employers is generally voluntary. Individuals have the right to keep their diagnosis private unless they choose to request accommodations.

2. When to Disclose: Some individuals may choose to disclose their ADHD diagnosis during the hiring process, while others may wait until they are established in their role. The decision to disclose is a personal one and should be based on individual comfort and needs.

Requesting Reasonable Accommodations

1. Initiating the Accommodation Process: To request accommodations, individuals typically need to initiate the process by informing their employer of their ADHD diagnosis and specifying the accommodations they require.

2. Interactive Process: The accommodation process is often interactive, involving a discussion between the employer and the individual to determine the most effective and reasonable accommodations.

Types of Reasonable Accommodations for ADHD

Organization and Time Management

1. Use of Organizational Tools: Providing access to organizational tools such as calendars, task lists, or project management software can assist individuals with ADHD in managing their workload effectively.

2. Structured Work Environment: Creating a structured work environment with clear guidelines and expectations can help individuals stay organized and focused on their tasks.

Flexible Work Arrangements

1. Flexible Work Hours: Allowing flexible work hours enables individuals to align their work with their peak focus times, potentially enhancing productivity and job performance.

2. Remote Work Options: Providing remote work options allows individuals to create a customized work environment, minimizing sensory distractions and optimizing concentration.

Breaks and Stress Management

1. Scheduled Breaks: Incorporating scheduled breaks into the workday enables individuals to manage stress and maintain focus, contributing to overall well-being.

2. Quiet or Designated Workspaces: Offering quiet or designated workspaces helps individuals with ADHD create an environment conducive to concentration.

Communication and Instructional Adjustments

1. Clear Communication Guidelines: Establishing clear communication guidelines, such as written

instructions or visual aids, assists individuals in understanding tasks and expectations.

2. Regular Check-Ins: Implementing regular check-ins between supervisors and employees fosters open communication, allowing for feedback and addressing any challenges.

Sensory Accommodations

1. Reducing Sensory Distractions: Modifying the work environment to reduce sensory distractions, such as minimizing noise or providing noise-canceling headphones, supports focus and concentration.

2. Adjusting Lighting: Making adjustments to lighting, such as using natural light or providing task lighting, can contribute to a more comfortable and visually friendly workspace.

Overcoming Challenges in Requesting Accommodations

## Stigma and Fear of Discrimination

1. Addressing Stigma: Encouraging open conversations about ADHD and neurodiversity in the workplace can contribute to reducing stigma. Promoting awareness and education helps create a more inclusive and understanding environment.

2. Educating Employers: Educating employers about ADHD and the benefits of neurodiversity can dispel misconceptions and foster a culture that values diverse perspectives and contributions.

## Advocacy for Legal Rights

1. Legal Assistance: Individuals facing challenges in securing accommodations or experiencing discrimination may seek legal assistance. Legal

professionals specializing in disability law can provide guidance and support.

2. Utilizing Internal Resources: Many organizations have internal resources, such as human resources departments or employee assistance programs, that can assist in navigating the legal rights and accommodations process.

Creating an Inclusive Workplace Culture

Training and Awareness Programs

1. Neurodiversity Training: Offering neurodiversity training programs for employees and supervisors raises awareness about ADHD and promotes understanding and acceptance in the workplace.

2. Sensitivity Training: Conducting sensitivity training helps colleagues understand the challenges

individuals with ADHD may face and fosters a supportive and empathetic work environment.

Inclusive Policies and Practices

1. Policy Development: Organizations can develop and implement inclusive policies that explicitly address the rights and accommodations of neurodivergent individuals, including those with ADHD.

2. Flexibility in Work Practices: Promoting flexibility in work practices, such as accommodating diverse communication styles or offering alternative work arrangements, contributes to a more inclusive workplace.

# Chapter 12

## Success Stories: Inspirational Journeys of ADHD Professionals

In this final chapter, we will look into the inspiring and triumphant stories of individuals with ADHD who have navigated the challenges of the professional world, showcasing resilience, determination, and success. These narratives highlight the diverse paths taken by ADHD professionals, illustrating how embracing neurodiversity and implementing supportive environments can lead to not only career success but also personal fulfillment.

Embracing Neurodiversity: The Foundation of Success

Sarah's Story: Thriving in a Creative Field

Sarah, a graphic designer, discovered her passion for art early in life. Diagnosed with ADHD as a child, she faced challenges in traditional educational settings but found solace in expressing herself through creative outlets. Her journey took a positive turn when she entered the workforce and joined a design agency that embraced neurodiversity. The organization provided a flexible work environment, recognizing the value of her unique perspectives and innovative thinking. Today, Sarah leads design projects, contributing to the agency's success while proving that neurodivergent individuals can excel in creative fields.

John's Journey: From Struggles to Entrepreneurial Success

John, diagnosed with ADHD in adolescence, faced academic struggles that continued into his early career. Despite setbacks, he discovered a keen interest in entrepreneurship. His turning point came when he founded his tech startup, leveraging his ADHD traits of hyperfocus and creativity. With a supportive team and a workplace culture that encouraged diverse thinking, his company flourished. His story showcases how embracing neurodiversity can lead to innovative solutions and entrepreneurial success.

Overcoming Academic Challenges: A Stepping Stone to Professional Triumph

Emma's Educational Odyssey: Navigating ADHD in Academia

Emma, a neuroscientist, faced challenges throughout her academic journey due to her ADHD. However, her passion for understanding the brain and neurodiversity fueled her determination. With support from mentors and accommodations such as extended deadlines, she excelled in her studies. Today, she leads groundbreaking research on ADHD, emphasizing the importance of accommodating diverse learning styles in academic settings.

Alex's Academic Pivot: Turning Challenges into Strengths

Alex, diagnosed with ADHD in college, initially struggled in a traditional academic environment. However, he discovered his strength in hands-on learning and problem-solving. Pursuing a career in a technical field, his ADHD traits became assets. His ability to hyperfocus and think outside the box propelled him into a successful career in software development. His story exemplifies the transformative power of adapting educational approaches to cater to diverse learning styles.

Navigating Corporate Labyrinths: Rising to the Top

Michelle's Climb: Breaking Glass Ceilings in Corporate America

Michelle, a high-ranking executive in a Fortune 500 company, faced gender and neurodiversity biases throughout her career. Diagnosed with ADHD early on, she embraced her differences and used her unique perspectives to drive innovation. With a strong support system and workplace accommodations, she shattered glass ceilings, emphasizing the importance of diversity at the highest levels of corporate leadership.

Daniel's Corporate Success: Leveraging ADHD Traits in Finance

Daniel, a finance professional diagnosed with ADHD, turned his challenges into strengths in the corporate world. His ability to hyperfocus allowed him to excel in data analysis, and his creative thinking led to innovative financial strategies. His success highlights how neurodivergent individuals can thrive in analytical fields when given the right support and accommodations.

Cultivating Supportive Work Environments: A Catalyst for Success

Maya's Workplace Transformation: Flourishing in a Supportive Culture

Maya, a marketing specialist, faced workplace challenges due to her ADHD until she joined a company that prioritized neurodiversity. The organization provided training for colleagues on ADHD awareness, flexible work arrangements, and quiet spaces. In this supportive environment, her productivity soared, and she became a key contributor to the company's marketing success. Her story emphasizes the impact of a neurodiverse workplace culture on individual and organizational success.

Building a Community: Connecting Through Shared Experiences

The ADHD Professionals Network: Fostering Community and Support

In response to the need for a supportive community, the ADHD Professionals Network was formed. Comprising individuals from various fields, this network offers a platform for sharing experiences, providing mentorship, and advocating for workplace accommodations. The stories within this network highlight the power of community in fostering professional growth and resilience.

## Online Platforms: Connecting Virtually for Support

In the digital age, online platforms have become essential for connecting neurodivergent professionals globally. Through forums, social media groups, and virtual events, individuals share advice, discuss workplace challenges, and celebrate successes. These online communities demonstrate the importance of virtual spaces in creating a sense of belonging and support for ADHD professionals.

## Advocacy and Awareness: Shaping the Future of Neurodiverse Workplaces

### Hannah Advocacy Journey: From Self-Advocacy to Industry Impact

Inspired by her personal journey, Hannah became an advocate for ADHD awareness in the workplace. She collaborates with organizations, sharing her story to dispel misconceptions and promote inclusivity. Her advocacy work illustrates the transformative power of individual voices in shaping more neurodiverse and empathetic workplaces.

### Corporate Initiatives: Leading the Way in Neurodiversity

Several corporations are taking proactive steps to promote neurodiversity. Through initiatives like targeted hiring programs, awareness campaigns, and mentorship opportunities, these companies are reshaping workplace cultures. By sharing success stories and championing inclusivity, they set a precedent for others to follow, fostering environments where individuals with ADHD can thrive.

## Conclusion

The stories of these ADHD professionals underscore the transformative power of embracing neurodiversity in the workplace. From overcoming academic challenges to rising to leadership positions, these individuals exemplify the potential for success when supported by inclusive environments and accommodations. Their journeys inspire not only neurodivergent individuals but also organizations and leaders to recognize the unique strengths that ADHD professionals bring to the table. By celebrating diversity, fostering understanding, and implementing supportive practices, workplaces can truly become spaces where every individual, regardless of neurodivergent status, can achieve fulfillment, contribute meaningfully, and reach their full potential.